WHSmith

Practice

Reading

Christine Moorcroft

Age 3–5
Year R
Early Years

Advice for parents

This book is designed for children to complete on their own but you will probably need to read the instructions on each page with them and check that they understand what to do. Some children, especially towards the younger end of the age range, will benefit from having the text read to or with them.

- Don't ask your child to do too much at once. A 'little and often' approach is a good way to start.
- Your child should work through the book unit by unit.
- Reward your child with lots of praise and encouragement.
- Talk to your child about what they have learned and what they can do.
- Some children will be able to read the texts for themselves but many will need help. They should read the text twice before answering any questions even if they read fluently.
- There are opportunities for all children to draw and write about what they have read, but some will need to answer the written questions orally.
- The '**Let's practise**' section consolidates understanding of the text.
- The '**How have I done?**' section provides some questions to help you to judge how well your child has read and understood the text. Read the instructions and questions with the child. Some questions have a space for writing one or more words. Where the answer is longer the child could answer orally. Some children could try writing longer answers even if they cannot spell all the words.
- The '**Teacher's tips**' are wriiten by practising classroom teachers. They give useful advice on specific topics or skills, to deepen your child's understanding and confidence and to help you help your child.
- The questions and activities begin at a simple level and become progressively more difficult towards the end of the unit. If your child finds them too difficult, read the text together and then help the child to answer orally.
- Answers and suggestions. Answers are provided where they might be helpful. There are also explanations to help your child and suggestions for making further use of the activity to develop his or her reading skills.

Reading skills

Literacy for children aged 3 to 5 comes under the broad headings of reading and writing. It is closely linked with a prime area of the Foundation Stage curriculum – communication and language. This includes listening and attention, understanding and speaking.

Children of this age group are expected to read and understand simple sentences and to use their phonic knowledge to decode regular words and read them aloud accurately, as well as reading some irregular words. They are expected to show understanding when talking to others about what they have read.

The link between reading and writing is very strong. Children who have learned to read fluently will make the most progress with their writing.

This book focuses on encouraging children to read different types of texts: stories, poems and rhymes, and everyday non-fiction texts such as labels, names and addresses and simple instructions.

Decoding words is addressed in another book in this series: *First Phonics Practice 3–5*.

Hachette UK's policy is to use papers that are natural, renewable and recyclable products and made from wood grown in sustainable forests. The logging and manufacturing processes are expected to conform to the environmental regulations of the country of origin.

Orders: please contact Bookpoint Ltd, 130 Milton Park, Abingdon, Oxon OX14 4SB. Telephone: (44) 01235 827720.
Fax: (44) 01235 400454. Lines are open 9.00a.m.–5.00p.m., Monday to Saturday, with a 24-hour message answering service.
Visit our website at www.hoddereducation.co.uk

First published in 2013 exclusively for WHSmith by
Hodder Education
An Hachette UK Company
338 Euston Road
London NW1 3BH

Impression number 10 9 8 7 6 5 4 3 2 1
Year 2018 2017 2016 2015 2014 2013

Cover illustration by Oxford Designers and Illustrators Ltd
All other illustrations Fakenham Prepress Solutions, Fakenham, Norfolk NR21 8NN
Typeset in Folio by Fakenham Prepress Solutions, Fakenham, Norfolk NR21 8NN
Printed in Italy

A catalogue record for this title is available from the British Library

ISBN: 978 1444 187 854

Contents

1: The Gingerbread Man

Once upon a time a lady made a big gingerbread man for her seven little boys.

She took the gingerbread man out of the oven.

He jumped off the baking tray. He ran out of the house and down the lane, calling,

'Run, run, as fast as you can. You can't catch me. I'm the gingerbread man.'

The lady ran after him. The seven little boys ran after him.

The cat ran after him. The hen ran after him. The little mouse ran after him.

The gingerbread man cried, 'Run, run, as fast as you can. You can't catch me. I'm the gingerbread man.'

Soon the gingerbread man came to a river. He couldn't get across.

A fox came and said, 'Jump onto my nose. I'll swim across the river and take you to the other side.'

So the gingerbread man jumped onto the fox's nose and called, 'Run, run, as fast as you can. You can't catch me. I'm the gingerbread man.'

Then the fox tossed the gingerbread man into the air. The fox opened his mouth. **And with a big SNAP of his teeth, he ate the gingerbread man.**

This is a traditional tale.

1. Use the pictures to help you to tell the story.

2. Now tell the story again.

This time, see if you can change the story. Give it a happy ending.

Teacher's tips

Read the story to your child more than once. As you read it, encourage your child to say the gingerbread man's words so that they can remember events. Remember the pictures are there as a reminder for your child.

2: Little Red Riding Hood

One day a little girl named Red Riding Hood went to see her grandma. Her grandma wasn't well, so she took some things for her: milk, bread and six apples.

Her mother called, 'Stay on the path. There is a wolf in the woods.'

But the wolf got into Grandma's house and ate Grandma. He put on her nightdress and nightcap and got into her bed.

Little Red Riding Hood went into the house.

'Grandma, what big ears you have!' she said.

'All the better to hear you with, my dear,' growled the wolf.

'Grandma, what big eyes you have!'

'All the better to see you with, my dear,' growled the wolf.

'Grandma, what big teeth you have!'

'All the better **TO EAT YOU WITH!'** roared the wolf. He jumped on Red Riding Hood and ate her.

Just then Red Riding Hood's father came. He was a woodman. He lifted his axe and cut off the wolf's head. He cut open the wolf and got Red Riding Hood and Grandma out.

1. Tick the things Red Riding Hood took to give Grandma:

2. Write what they said:

3. What happened next?

Teacher's tips

As you read the story, draw your child's attention to the items Little Red Riding Hood takes with her. Have these items on a table so that your child can put them in a basket. This will make question 1 easier.

3: The Little Red Hen

The Little Red Hen said, 'I shall make a cake.'
'Who will help me to cut this wheat?' asked the Little Red Hen.
'Not I!' said the cat.
'Not I!' said the duck.
'Not I!' said the mouse.
'Then I shall cut it myself,' said the Little Red Hen.

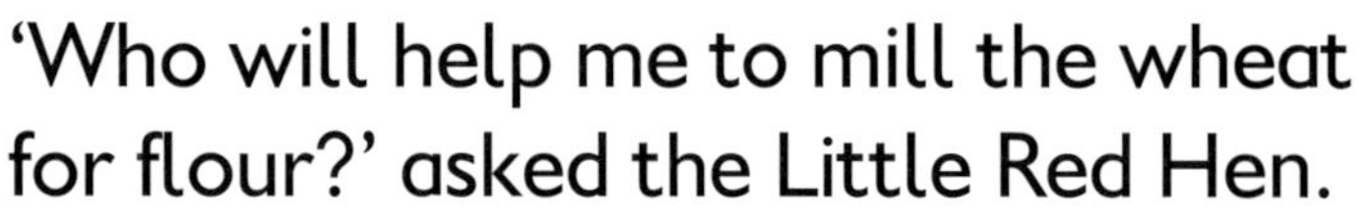

'Who will help me to mill the wheat for flour?' asked the Little Red Hen.
'Not I!' said the cat.
'Not I!' said the duck.
'Not I!' said the mouse.
'Then I shall mill it myself,' said the Little Red Hen.

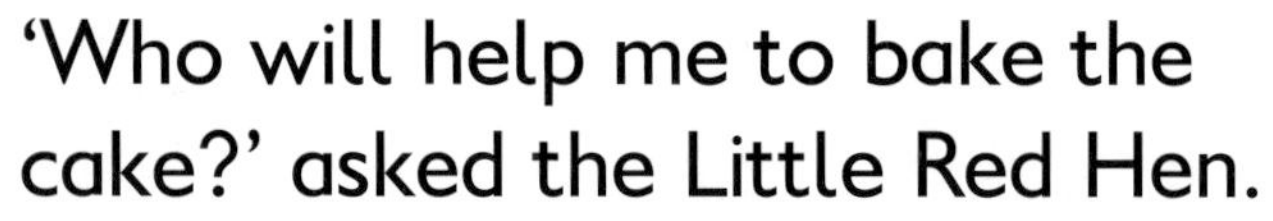

'Who will help me to bake the cake?' asked the Little Red Hen.
'Not I!' said the cat.
'Not I!' said the duck.
'Not I!' said the mouse.
'Then I shall bake it myself,' said the Little Red Hen.

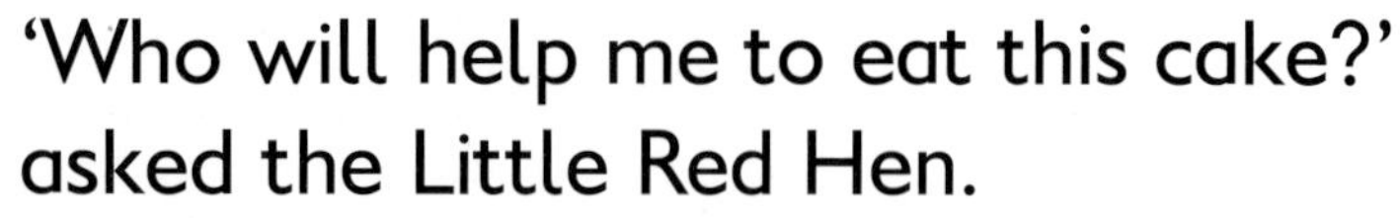

'Who will help me to eat this cake?' asked the Little Red Hen.
'I will,' said the cat.
'I will,' said the duck.
'I will,' said the mouse.
'No you won't. I shall eat it myself,' said the Little Red Hen.

Let's practise

1. What did the Little Red Hen make? ✓

bread ☐

ice cream ☐

a cake ☐

chips ☐

2. Did they help? Write yes or no.

____________ ____________ ____________

3. Did the cat, duck and mouse want to help eat the cake?
   Write yes or no.

____

4. What did the Little Red Hen say?

____

____

Teacher's tips

Read the story twice to your child. Emphasise the words ***duck, mouse*** and ***cat*** as you read. You could have ***Yes*** and ***No*** cards ready so that as each animal says ***No*** or ***Yes*** your child can hold up the appropriate card.

4: This is a house for me

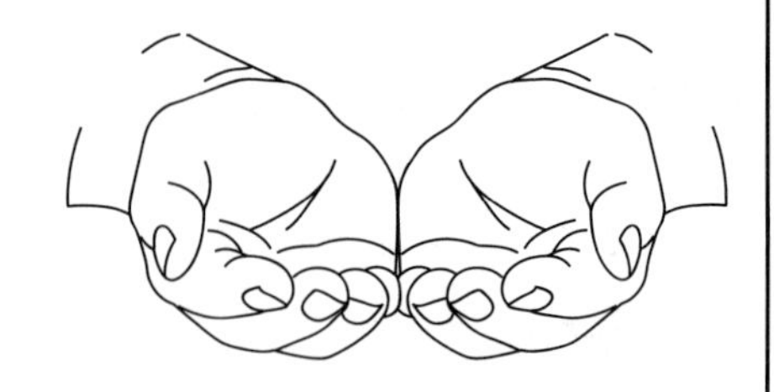

This is a nest for a blackbird.

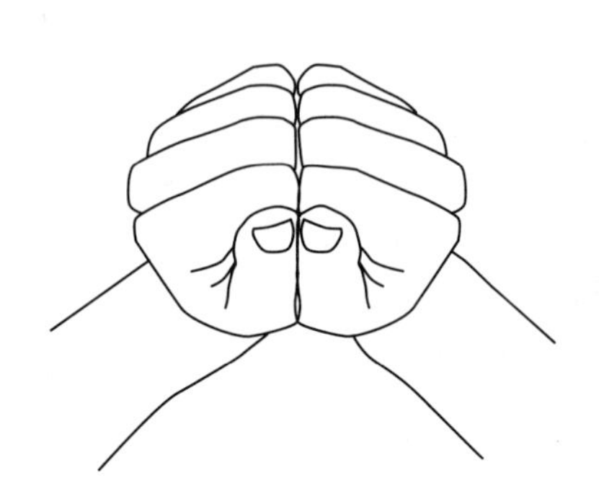

This is a hive for a bee.

This is a hole for a rabbit.

And this is a house for me!

Let's practise

This is an action rhyme.

1. Look at the pictures.
   Read the rhyme and do the actions.
2. Cover the words.
   Look at the pictures and say the rhyme.
3. Now try without looking at the pictures.
4. Draw lines to match the animals to the houses.

5. Write the missing words.

This is a ________________ for a ________________.

This is a ________________ for a ________________.

This is a ________________ for a ________________.

And this is a ________________ for ________________!

Teacher's tips

If your child finds question 5 difficult write the words ***house, hive, hole*** and ***nest*** on card or paper. Read each word to your child and ask them where it needs to go.

5: Higgledy Piggledy Pop

Higgledy piggledy pop
The duck has eaten the mop.
The cow's in a hurry,
The cat's in a flurry
Higgledy piggledy pop.

This is an old rhyme.
No one knows who wrote it.
It is a funny poem.
It has just one verse.
It has five lines.
It has lines that rhyme.

Let's practise

1. Read the poem with someone to help.
   Read it again, with help.
   See if you can remember the words.
   Now try to say the poem by yourself.

These pictures will help!

2. Who ate the mop? ✓

   cat ☐ cow ☐ duck ☑

3. Who is in a hurry?

   cat ☐ cow ☑ duck ☐

4. Who is in a flurry?

   cat ☑ cow ☐ duck ☐

5. Make up your own verse. Choose words that rhyme. Write them in the gaps.

Higgledy piggledy pips
The duck has eaten the mop.
The cow's in a muddle,
The cat's in a flurry
Higgledy piggledy pop.

Teacher's tips

Read the verse over a few times. Your child may be able to memorise it. As you read, point out the animal words so that question 1 is easier. Remind your child that whatever the duck eats in question 5 must rhyme with *pips*!

6: The Park

I'm glad that I

Live near a park

For in the winter

After dark

The park lights shine

As bright and still

As dandelions

On a hill.

James S. Tippett

This poem has just one verse.
It has only eight lines.
It is a quiet poem.
The poet wants us to read it slowly.
He splits it into short lines.
This makes us read it slowly.

Let's practise

1. Listen to someone reading the poem.
   Then ask them to read it again.
   This time you join in.

2. Tick the words that describe the poem: ✓

   exciting ☐ quiet ☑ noisy ☐

   happy ☑ sad ☐ boring ☐

3. Is the poem about a park at night or in the daytime?

   ____

4. Which season is it in the poem? ✓

   spring ☐ summer ☑ autumn ☐ winter ☑

5. Write words in the poem that rhyme with these:

   park ______________ still ______________

Teacher's tips

For question 5, have the words ***ark*** and ***ill*** on two pieces of card. Using consonant letter/phoneme cards you can show your child the words ***p+ark*** and ***st+ill***. Help them to form new rhyming words by replacing the starting consonants letters/ phonemes.

7: Shopping

There are a lot of shops in Main Street.
May, Matt and Tia are going shopping. They are going to Main Street. They have shopping lists. They go on the bus.

Let's practise

Here are May, Matt and Tia's shopping lists:

May

bread
stamps
flowers

Matt

cake
sweets
a hat

Tia

a toy car
chops
a jumper

1. Who buys sweets? Matt
2. Who buys chops? Tia
3. Who buys stamps? May
4. Which shops does May go to? ✓

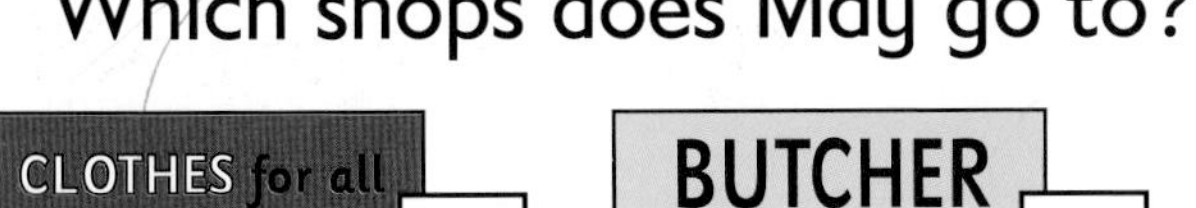

POST OFFICE ✓

Toys for You

TED'S sweet shop

Teacher's tips

Spend some time talking about the different shops in the picture and discuss what each might sell. Draw your child's attention to the words ***sweets, chops*** and ***stamps*** as you read over the items May, Matt and Tia list.

8: The Postman

Here is the postman.
The postman takes the letters to Well Lane.
Here are the letters.

Let's practise

Here are the houses in Well Lane.

1. Write the people's names on their houses.
2. How many houses are there in Well Lane? 4
3. Who lives at 1 Well Lane? Tim Pay
4. What number is Zak Coe's house? 4
5. Who lives next door to Bal Singh? Zak Coe

Teacher's tips

You can make these pages more real. Have some labelled envelopes and pictures of numbered houses ready. Create a street on the floor or table with your house pictures. Your child can be the postman as they complete the activities!

9: Chocolate crispies

How to make chocolate crispies

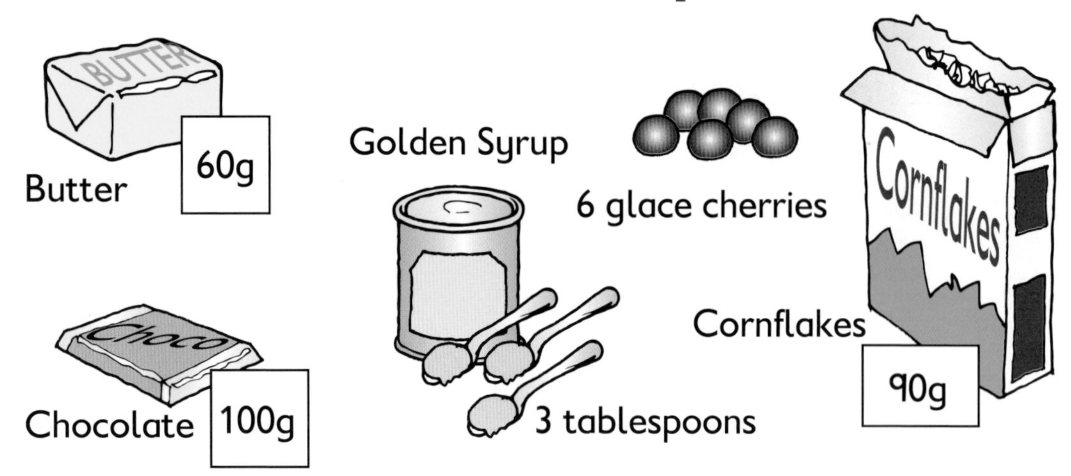

1. Wash your hands.

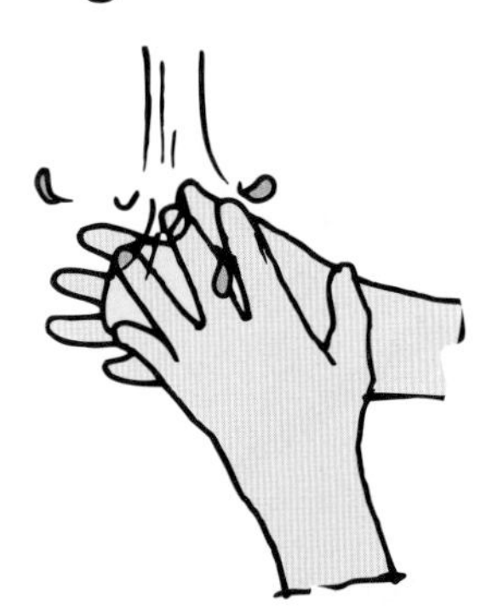

2. Put on an apron.

3. Melt the butter, syrup and chocolate.

4. Mix in the cornflakes.

5. Put the mixture into six cake cases.

6. Put a cherry on top.

Let's practise

You can make chocolate crispies.
Ask a grown-up to help.
Fill in the gaps.

1. Wash your ________________.

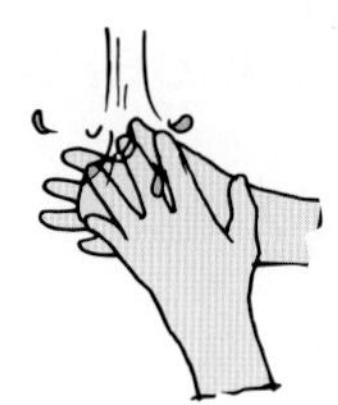

2. Put on an ________________.

3. Melt the ________________,

   ________________ and chocolate.

4. ________________ in the cornflakes.

5. Put the mixture into

   ________________ cases.

6. Put a ________________ on top.

7. What will you do next? ________________________________

   ____

Teacher's tips

Spend some time thinking about the importance of being able to read a recipe thoroughly before beginning to cook. Otherwise the results might be a disaster!

How have I done?

Here are some questions for you to talk about.
Look at the other pages in this book to help you.

1. What did the gingerbread man say?
2. Who ate the gingerbread man?
3. Who said this?

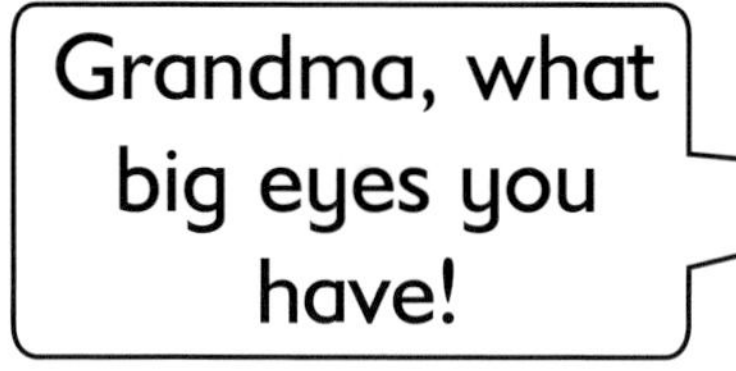

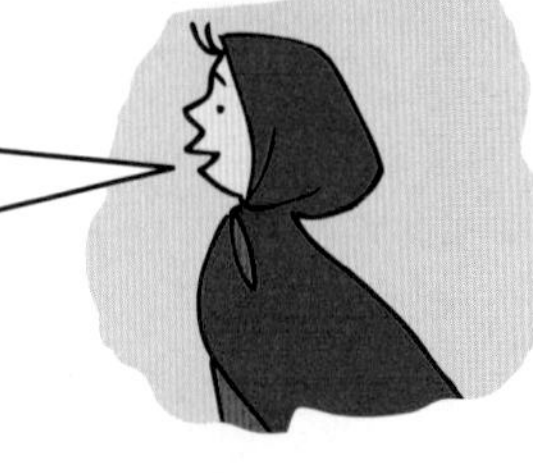

4. The Little Red Hen said, 'Who will help me to bake the cake?' What did the other animals say?

5. Say the rhyme 'This is a house for me'. Do the actions. Write the missing words.

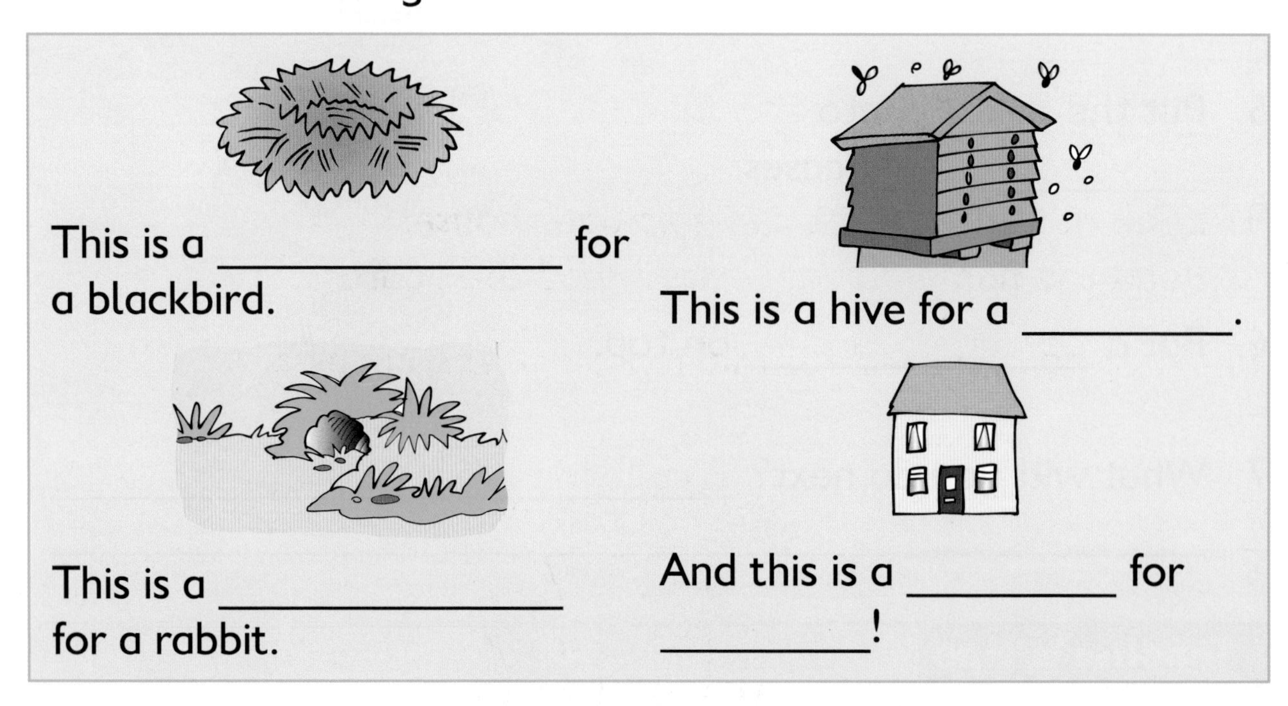

This is a ________________ for a blackbird.

This is a hive for a __________.

This is a ________________ for a rabbit.

And this is a __________ for __________!

6. Write the missing word.

Higgledy piggledy pop
The duck is eating the ______________.

7. Write the missing word from the poem 'The Park':
   I'm glad that I
   Live near a ______________

8. Read the shopping list.
   Which shops will Tam go to?

Tam's shopping list

Shirt
Cake
Meat

9. Look at a letter that came to your house.
   Read the name on the letter. Read the address.

10. What do you need for making chocolate crispies?

Answers and suggestions

UNIT 1
Read the story with the child, pointing to the words. Encourage them to join in, especially with the repeated words 'Run, run, as fast as you can. You can't catch me. I'm the gingerbread man.' Let the child re-tell the story in their own way, using the pictures to help. Talk about how to change it for a happy ending.

UNIT 2
Read the story with the child, pointing to the words. Encourage them to join in, especially with the repeated words 'Grandma, what big ...' and 'All the better to ...' Re-read parts, if necessary, to help the child to answer the questions:
1. milk, bread, apples; 2. 'All the better to eat you with.'

UNIT 3
Read the story with the child, pointing to the words. Encourage them to join in, especially with the repeated words 'Who will help ...?' and 'Not I!' Talk about the windmill and what it was for. Read the questions with the child.
1. a cake; 2. No (for all); 3. Yes; 4. 'No you won't. I shall eat it myself.'

UNIT 4
Read the action rhyme with the child, showing the actions. Encourage them to join in with the actions and words.
5. nest, blackbird; hive, bee; hole, rabbit; house, me.

UNIT 5
Read the rhyme with the child, pointing to the words, emphasising the rhyming words. Encourage them to join in.
2. duck; 3. cow; 4. cat; 5. Any suitable rhyme: e.g.
Higgledy piggledy pips
The duck has eaten the chips
The cow's in a muddle,
The cat's in a puddle
Higgledy piggledy pips.

UNIT 6
Read the rhyme with the child. The verse structure encourages slow, measured reading and a gentle voice.
2. quiet, happy; 3. night (Point out that it says 'after dark' and describes the lights shining in the dark.); 4. winter; 5. dark, hill

UNIT 7
Talk about the picture and help the child to read the signs. If necessary, read the introduction with them, and read the shopping lists.
1. Matt; 2. Tia; 3. May; 4 baker, post office, Rosie's Flowers

UNIT 8
If necessary, help the child to read the introduction, names and addresses.
1. Number 1 Tim Day, Number 2 Ann Lee, Number 3 Bal Sing, Number 4 Zak Lee; 2. 4; 3. Tim Day; 4. 4; 5. Zak Coe.

UNIT 9
Talk about the heading. Tell the child that this is a recipe – instructions for making chocolate crispies. If possible, follow the recipe with the child to make some.
1. hands; 2. apron; 3. butter, syrup; 4. Mix; 5. cake; 6. cherry; 7. Any suitable answer: e.g. *Eat it* or *Give it to ...*

HOW HAVE I DONE?
1. 'Run, run, as fast as you can. You can't catch me. I'm the gingerbread man.'; 2. The fox; 3. Little Red Riding Hood; 4. 'Not I!'; 5. nest, bee, hole, house, me; 6. mop; 7. park; 8. clothes shop, baker, butcher; 9. Show the child an envelope addressed to someone they know at their home address.; 10. chocolate, syrup, butter, cornflakes, cherries